Museums & Galleries Commission

REPORT ON THE NATIONAL MUSEUMS

To:

The Right Honourable Richard Luce MP,
Minister for the Arts

The Right Honourable Peter Walker MBE MP,
Secretary of State for Wales

The Right Honourable Tom King MP,
Secretary of State for Northern Ireland

The Right Honourable Malcolm Rifkind QC MP,
Secretary of State for Scotland

On behalf of the Commission I have the honour to submit our report on the national museums and galleries of the United Kingdom. Chapter 1 explains its purpose, and Chapter 7 restates our conclusions.

I am sending a copy of the report to the Secretaries of State for Defence and for the Environment, in view of their responsibilities for certain of the national museums.

Brian Morris, Chairman

Peter Longman, Secretary
7 St James's Square, 6 April 1988

Museums & Galleries Commission

Contents

1. Introduction

This is above all a report of ideas and principles. We say what the national museums and galleries are; what makes them important and entitled to substantial public funding; and what opportunities and duties and problems they have in common. Our report is addressed to the national museums themselves, to museums generally and to the interested public; but especially to the Ministers whom it is our duty to advise. We believe that what we say is relevant to the formulation of attitudes and policies, and will help to provide a basis for decisions.

There has been no official report on the national museums collectively for almost 60 years (in 1929 a Royal Commission reported on those in London and Edinburgh). Since then there have been great changes. In particular, the last ten years have seen many developments in museum activity and finance, and in the relationship between museums, the Government and the public. For these reasons we decided that the time was right for a general review. We have undertaken it as the only body with an overview of museums throughout the United Kingdom; and from our position of quasi-independence, distanced from both the Government and the national museums.

The field is huge, and we have had to be selective. We focus on a number of issues that seem to us especially important. Some are painfully familiar. Others, we think, have received less attention than they deserve: notably the importance of scholarship, the limitations of private funding, and the role of Trustees.

We have visited every museum, and discussed its achievements, problems and plans with the Director and some of the Trustees. We have drawn on these discussions for examples to illustrate our conclusions. But we are conscious that by generalising, and avoiding issues that are the concern of a single Trustee body, we have not done justice to individual museums; to the marvellous places they are to visit; to the astonishing range of their collections; to the splendid buildings most of them occupy. Nor have we said how many of their roofs leak.

In Chapters 2–6 that follow, we discuss the distinctive features of national museums, how they are funded, governed, controlled, directed and staffed, and some aspects of their collections. In Chapter 7 we restate our main conclusions.

Throughout the report, a reference to the national museums or a national museum should be taken as meaning the national museums and galleries, or one of them.

1

2. The Nature of a National Museum

The National Museums

The terms of reference of the Royal Commission in 1927 rather begged the question of what were the national museums by defining them as those containing the national collections. We prefer not to follow this path, for in a sense the national collections comprise all those in any kind of public ownership or trusteeship.

We prefer to talk of national museums and their collections. Since there is no statutory definition of a national museum,[1] it will be as well to make clear at the outset the museums which our report covers. They are:

British Museum
British Museum (Natural History)
Imperial War Museum
National Army Museum
National Gallery
National Maritime Museum
National Museums and Galleries on Merseyside
National Portrait Gallery
Royal Air Force Museum
Royal Armouries
Science Museum
Tate Gallery
Victoria & Albert Museum
Wallace Collection
National Galleries of Scotland
National Museums of Scotland
National Museum of Wales
Ulster Folk and Transport Museum
Ulster Museum

---

[1] The nearest approach to a statutory definition of a national museum is in the National Gallery and Tate Gallery Act 1954. Schedule 1 contains a list of museums, which is varied from time to time by statutory instrument. At present it comprises 12 of the 19 we have listed. Together with the National Gallery and the Tate Gallery, these are the only ones in which the Minister may vest works of art given or bequeathed to the nation (he is not so restricted in allocating items accepted in lieu of tax). They are also the museums to which the Tate Gallery, British Museum, British Museum (Natural History), Royal Armouries, Science Museum and the V & A Museum may transfer objects from their collections.

They total nineteen. Fourteen of them are in England (all but one with their main building in London), two in Scotland, and two in Northern Ireland, and one is in Wales.

The rationale for inclusion in the list varies. The Royal Armouries can claim to be the oldest national collection, having been open to the general public since the time of Charles II and to special visitors since the reign of Henry VIII. It is the only one of our national museums (unlike many of those in continental Europe) to be of royal origin. The British Museum is the oldest institution, and the oldest Trustee body, having been established by Act of Parliament in 1753.

A hallmark of a national museum has always been its funding by the Exchequer. Whether vested in Trustees at the outset (as with the British Museum) or originally set up as a departmental museum (as with the Science Museum), the Government assumed full funding responsibility. The same was true of the components of the present National Galleries of Scotland and National Museums of Scotland, when they were established as national institutions in the mid-19th century; and of the Wallace Collection, when it was bequeathed to the nation in 1897; and of the National Museum of Wales, when it was established in 1907 and granted a Royal Charter[1] in 1911. The same was true, too, of the two national museums established between the two world wars: the Imperial War Museum in 1920 and the National Maritime Museum in 1934.

The last thirty years have seen the establishment as national museums of five that we have listed: the National Army Museum and the Royal Air Force Museum; the two national museums of Northern Ireland; and lastly the National Museums and Galleries on Merseyside, established by Order in 1986 because it appeared to the Minister that, in the words of the Act,[2] 'their collections were of such national importance that they should be vested in Trustees and supported by moneys provided by Parliament'.

Characteristics of National Museums

The national museums we have listed have four characteristics in common: their collections are of national importance in terms of the United Kingdom or of a part of the United Kingdom; they are vested in Trustees on the nation's behalf; they are wholly or mainly funded directly by the Government; and the Government is able to call on their staff from time to time for such expert advice in their field as it may require.

---

[1] The Royal Charter provides for the National Museum of Wales to operate under a Court of Governors. In this report, references to Trustees should be taken to apply *mutatis mutandis* to the Court of Governors or its Council.

[2] Local Government Act 1985, section 46

Various other museums, which might be considered national by reason of their status or of the importance of their collections, do not have all these characteristics and are not covered by this report: university museums (owned by universities and largely funded through them by the University Grants Committee); the Public Record Office Museum and other departmental museums (such as the Prison Service Museum); regimental and corps museums and the various Royal Navy museums (the Fleet Air Museum, the Royal Naval Museum, the Submarine Museum and the Royal Marines Museum, which are not on the same single-service footing as the National Army Museum or the Royal Air Force Museum); Sir John Soane's Museum (still owned by a private Trust); the Museum of London (half funded by the City of London). Our report does not cover the museums of economic botany, which are no longer a separate entity within the Royal Botanic Gardens at Kew. Nor does it deal with the National Libraries of Scotland and Wales; though covered by previous Commission reports and faced with many of the same problems, they are different in nature from national museums.

The word National in a museum's name does not of course, in this context, necessarily signify national status. For example, the well-established independent National Motor Museum in Beaulieu, which holds the leading national collection of cars, is not a national museum in the sense of this report. On the other hand we have, as a Commission, been concerned at instances where the word National in a museum's name has been misused (for example the National Butterfly Museum in Sussex was neither national nor a museum); and our forthcoming museum registration scheme will contain safeguards against this misuse.

Importance of National Museums

Together, the national museums' collections are of the highest international importance, unrivalled in their range and diversity, as in their quality. To a great extent they represent the patronage, discernment and generosity of generations of benefactors. Charting the extent of human knowledge and achievement in every branch of art and science, with specimens and artefacts and works of art from every part of the world, they reflect the nation's place in the history of civilisation. They are part of the nation's patrimony, to be used and enjoyed and built upon now, and to be sustained for the future. As large tourist attractions – their combined attendances last year (see Table 1) were nearly 26 million – they are an economic asset of significant national importance.

National Museums Further Distinguished

In considering what are the additional characteristics of national museums and what is their special role in the nation's life, over and above the duty of their Trustees and staff to care for the national collections and allow public access to them, we have concluded that each national museum has, or should have, two further distinctive features. First, it should excel in scholarship and use its collections for the advancement of learning. Second, it should exhibit its collections so as to provide the widest public benefit. These two duties are well summarised in the first Statutes and Rules of the British Museum, published in 1759: 'though chiefly designed for the use of learned and studious men, both natives and foreigners, in their researches into the several parts of knowledge, yet being a national establishment . . . it may be judged reasonable that the advantages accruing from it should be rendered as general as possible'. We discuss these duties in turn below.

Scholarship

The Commission's Report on Museums in Scotland[1] called the national museums the intellectual hub of the museum system. It is equally true to say that the intellectual activities of national museums are central to their other purposes. They were founded essentially as institutions for education and research (and both the British Museum and the National Gallery were publicly funded several years before any school or university received public funding). They seek to sustain their collections, and to promote the learning based upon them, so as to serve scholars worldwide. For well over 200 years this concept has attracted men and women of high quality into the service of national museums, informed their thinking and dictated their attitudes. These collections are part of the history of ideas, their curators a species of historian. Their scholarship must be of a quality that commands the respect of others working in the field, in universities and elsewhere. Indeed much of the research in national museums – for example, the scientific research undertaken by the British Museum (Natural History), and the conservation research undertaken by the British Museum – is essential in the context of university work. Clearly some national museums are better able than others to pursue scholarly research based on their collections, but each should undertake some. Indeed, if any were to fail entirely in this respect, it would ultimately forfeit its claim to be regarded as a national museum.

---

[1] Museums in Scotland: Report by a Working Party of the Museums and Galleries Commission (HMSO, 1986)

The national museums of the United Kingdom have an international reputation for academic excellence. In taxonomy, their contribution to world classification systems is outstanding. Their record of scholarly publications and catalogues is impressive. Here are some examples. In 1984, staff of the British Museum published, *inter alia*, its catalogues of Egyptian Antiquities, French Medals, European Scientific Instruments and Western Asiatic Seals. In 1985, staff of what are now the National Museums of Scotland published, *inter alia*, a detailed and critical assessment of prehistoric European artefacts regarded as power symbols, and books on French art collected by Scots, and on Kuwaiti artefacts and culture. And in 1986, among numerous publications by staff of the V & A Museum, were books on Heraldic Symbols, and on Chinese Dress; and staff of the British Museum (Natural History) published nine specialist books, three scholarly catalogues and over 400 papers in learned journals.

In some fields, the research effort takes the form of innovation and experiment. Here we may instance the British Museum's Lindow Man project; the National Gallery's pioneering work in conservation science; and the documentation of collections by the National Museums of Scotland.

This scholarly activity is a major part of the work of senior curators and conservators in a national museum. They are expected to be experts in their field, internationally regarded as authorities. To do their job properly and maintain their international reputation, they need time for research; they must keep abreast of their subject, visit other collections, read widely, contribute to publications, attend conferences and seminars, and play a leading part in their academic community. This research and this sort of scholarly activity are not luxuries, to be cut when money is scarce. They are fundamental to the role and purpose of a great museum.

We have been concerned to find that in every national museum, in every field, scholarship and the associated excellence of curatorial standards are perceived as being increasingly under threat. Shortage of money, the downward pressure on staff numbers, the extra time curators need to spend on managerial tasks, and their move to service functions, are seen as combining to erode the time they have for scholarly activities. At a time when increased emphasis is properly given to management and marketing, the crucial importance of research and scholarship in national museums needs to be stressed again. The influence of the national museums, moreover, goes far beyond their own walls, for they are the pacemakers; other important museums look to them for leadership in scholarship, as in other respects. In a national museum, the fostering and upholding of excellence are as much a duty as maintaining the fabric and balancing the books.

Widest Public Benefit

The National Heritage Act 1983 requires the Trustees of the V & A Museum, to take one example, to see that their collections are exhibited to the public, and 'generally to promote the public's enjoyment and understanding of art, craft and design, both by means of the Board's collections and by such other means as they consider appropriate'.

A national museum's duty to exhibit and to promote public enjoyment and understanding is given effect both within and outside the museum. We pay special attention here to what might be done outside. Individual national museums already do much to project themselves outside the capital cities, to other museums and the wider public. We mention below a number of ways in which this projection is made, and suggest what more might be done.

First, many national museums have branches, mostly outside the capital cities. The Appendices list a total of 45, of which no fewer than eleven have been opened in the last ten years, representing a considerable regional thrust. For example, the Science Museum has large satellite museums, with major specialist collections, in York and Bradford. The National Portrait Gallery displays parts of its collections in National Trust houses in Somerset and Yorkshire; another display will be opened in Clwyd in July, in collaboration with the county council. And the National Museum of Wales has always taken seriously its cardinal duty to project itself by means of branch museums. In the planning of further branches, national museums should consult with other interests – for example, on possible inner city sites. National museums may have a part to play in urban regeneration, in economic as well as educational terms; but, even where capital may be available, they should be careful to secure running costs before committing themselves to establishing a provincial centre.

Second, national collections can, like other collections, now include objects or works of art which come into the museum's ownership but remain *in situ*. Such objects and works can, for example, be accepted in lieu of tax on condition that they remain in the house with which they have long been associated. In the science field, comparable arrangements might be made, for example, in the case of industrial archaeological sites. We see scope for extending the idea of national museums developing special relationships with regional locations, short of opening more outstations.

Third, there is growing pressure for national museums to adopt a more positive policy towards loans to museums in the regions and towards travelling exhibitions. We suggest that, in future, national museums should automatically consider the travelling potential of each exhibition they organise. Not every such exhibition will be able to travel, but those which do so might recover the marginal costs, particularly transport costs, from the locations visited. Where a national museum wished to charge more than marginal costs, the museums visited would become partners, sharing in the exhibition's selection and promotion, as well as in its costs. In these cases the Commission might consider using its limited travelling exhibition funds to help the non-national partner.

Fourth, national museums might do more to help with the training of specialist staff from those other museums which can spare them. We develop this point in Chapter 5.

Fifth, national museums generously provide information and *ad hoc* advice in certain fields now, but it is important that smaller and medium-sized museums generally should feel able to draw upon the specialised expertise available in the national museums – for example, in scientific analytical research – as well as for general advice and moral support. Many museums are now in local authority leisure Departments that may not place a high value on academic expertise. National museum staff need the time to give help when local museums need it, for example in identifying museum material. In this context, a recent Commission report[1] noted the impression that in Scotland the national museums' relations with other museums were more extensive and cordial than elsewhere in the United Kingdom. We believe that every national museum has an opportunity for developing its relations with other museums, and that mutual understanding of each other's needs and resources would develop from further visits and occasional one-day discussions and seminars. The flow of information need not be always in one direction: some staff in local museums are more in tune with modern developments than some in national museums.

Sixth, there is scope for a national museum to give a lead in co-ordinating the approach of other museums operating in its field. For example, the National Maritime Museum is taking the initiative by inviting other maritime museums to co-operate in sharing information and experience.

Seventh, we should like to think that, when a national museum is making plans to computerise the catalogues and inventories of its collections, it will take account of the probable future needs of other museums. We return to this point in Chapter 6.

Eighth and last, there are opportunities for the national museums to forge closer links with universities and other educational institutions, and to extend their national role by developing education and open-learning programmes. Television will clearly be an important medium in this context.

[1] Museums in Scotland (HMSO, 1986)

Summary

National museums have a characteristic duty to promote public understanding and enjoyment. They have come under increasing pressure to implement this principle in terms of heightened attraction and entertainment. This is no bad thing: some move in this direction was certainly needed. But the national museums' success must rest on more than their popularity. In our view this means their reasserting the key importance of scholarship as a priority, and consciously accepting a responsibility for developing closer relations with local museums, reaching out in a positive way and allowing their collections to benefit the widest public. Clearly their ability to act in this way will depend to some extent on their funding, to which we turn in the next chapter.

3. Funding the National Museums

Public Funding

Until the present decade, no one doubted that the Government accepted full financial responsibility for the national museums, whether they were run by an Education Department or by Trustees. This responsibility is not, however, fully reflected in recent legislation. For example, the National Heritage Act 1983 provides, in the case of the V & A Museum and the Science Museum, that any expenditure incurred by the Trustees 'shall, except so far as defrayed out of other sources, be defrayed out of money provided by Parliament'. And the same 1983 Act provides, in the case of the Trustees of the Royal Armouries, that the Secretary of State 'may out of money provided by Parliament pay . . . such sums towards their expenditure as the Treasury may approve'. This wording appears also in the 1986 Order constituting the National Museums and Galleries on Merseyside. It is clear that the Government can now claim to have discretion as to how much to contribute to a national museum's approved expenditure.

Tables 3, 4 and 5 show Government funding of each of the national museums – for running costs, in purchase grants, and in total – in each of the last ten years, from 1979–80 to the current year 1988–89.

Table 3 shows Government funding for *Running Costs*. These comprise general administrative expenditure, between 70% and 80% of which is made up of staff costs. Most of the 1988–89 figures show a sharp increase since, following the change to grant-in-aid status, they include substantial sums for pension contributions and other Government services not previously shown on museum votes. For this reason, we consider here only the figures from 1979–80 to 1987–88 (and exclude the National Museums and Galleries on Merseyside, which were directly funded only from 1986–87). Over this period, total Government funding for running costs increased by 27% in real terms (using the GDP deflator). But during this period the national museums' commitments were growing: eleven branch museums were opened after 1979, and their total staff numbers increased by 8% between 1977 and 1987. Moreover, the increases in funding have since 1981–82 consistently fallen below trends in the levels of civil service pay settlements (which dictate the pay of national museum staff but, being negotiated between Government and civil service staff associations, are outside the museums' control). The funding gap is clearly shown in the chart opposite:

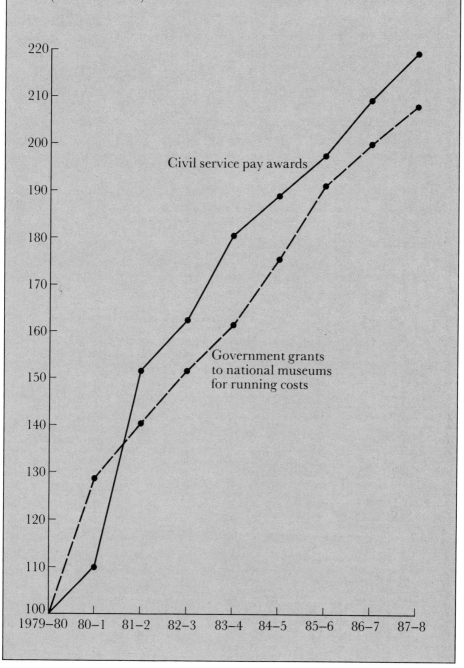

Indices of Government grants to national museums (excluding the National Museums and Galleries on Merseyside) for running costs, and of civil service pay awards for administrative grades (1979–80 = 100)

Civil service pay awards

Government grants to national museums for running costs

This funding gap is serious, and has had adverse consequences in all the national museums, which have had to leave unfilled varying numbers of posts in their complements (though these were determined after Government staff inspections). The effects are lamentably to be seen in terms of closed galleries, reduced security, curtailed opening hours or days (as at the V & A until recently), backlogs of work (eg on conservation and the production of catalogues and other scholarly publications), less ability to help schools (especially now, with GCSE), inefficient use of staff time (word-processors can hardly be afforded), and less good service to the public (for example, the National Art Library at the V & A is still closed one day a week, and sorely underfunded). Most serious is the danger of a cumulative, long-term decline in curatorial standards, as reduced staff are increasingly stretched and often unable to maintain contact with other international scholars, find time to attend international gatherings, take necessary study leave or publish accumulated experience.

The *Purchase Grant* figures in Table 4 show a general pattern of modest cash increases until 1983–84 but, at least in the case of the national museums funded by the Office of Arts & Libraries (OAL), none at all since then. This reflects OAL's policy of freezing purchase grants in order to provide more money for building maintenance. For example, the National Gallery's present purchase grant is, in purchasing power, worth barely half that of its grant ten years ago. It is fair to add that during the period the ability of several national museums to add to their collections was enhanced by grants from the National Heritage Memorial Fund for certain items from the United Kingdom's heritage (see Table 6); and also by the allocation of certain items accepted by the Government in lieu of tax.

In Table 5, which gives total grants to the national museums, money for the *Buildings* of those in Cardiff and Belfast and on Merseyside, which have never used the Government's Property Services Agency (PSA), is included in each year's figures. For those in London untied from the PSA this year, generally only the 1988–89 figures include money for buildings, as detailed in each Appendix (those in Edinburgh are to be untied from the PSA next year). Where the PSA was responsible for national buildings, funding Departments transferred block amounts to the PSA (and – deplorably, in our view – allocations to individual museums are not published). In 1979–80, these totalled some £15m; in 1987–88, some £35m, representing an increase of 34% in real terms (using the GDP deflator). This year, 1988–89, the Government's provision for *all* the national museums' buildings amounts to some £56m. In general, we welcome the emphasis the Government has given in recent years to money for national museum buildings. Each Board of Trustees now responsible for its buildings will no doubt be arranging surveys of

12

them; these will show whether or not the forecast provision will be enough to put and keep them in reasonable order.

Plural Funding

Plural funding is central to the Government's policy. Publicly funded bodies are encouraged to raise more money themselves. We approve. The national museums have practised plural funding for years. They have sold books, advice and services; received donations and bequests; and charged for admission to certain exhibitions. And we applaud the Government's decision two years ago to let them keep all the money they receive, which has given them an incentive to increase their trading, improve their catering and enlarge their publication programmes. We welcome these developments. Recreation is part of the experience of visiting a museum; appropriate commercial activities – those which do not detract from the museum's essential function – are to be encouraged; and donations and sponsorship are to be welcomed as an additional source of funds for capital projects.

We see plural funding as a means of increasing a national museum's total revenue, to enable it to improve its service to the public. The Government claims to do the same: the Minister for the Arts has said[1] that he aims 'to maintain the level of support from public funds [for the arts as a whole], but to encourage subsidised bodies to become more self-reliant in their development and growth'. This is his declared aim. The reality is different. Faced with shortfalls in Government funding, national museums have had to raise money to avoid cutting essential staff. They are having to become self-reliant to keep going.

Last year, for example, the British Museum (Natural History) – then funded by the Department of Education and Science through the Advisory Board for the Research Councils – decided to introduce admission charges to cover the shortfall in Government funding. The alternative would have been a reduction of 75 scientific staff over five years. Trustees should be free to decide to introduce admission charges, if they judge this right, as a means of producing extra revenue to improve the museum's service to the public. They ought not to be put in the position of having to introduce charges to pay for essential staff.

[1] House of Commons Official Report, 5 November 1987

The Future of Public Funding

Before considering, in their corporate planning, how they can generate supplementary revenue, the national museums first need a secure base of public funding. They need to be able to look ahead with confidence. In this context we warmly welcome last year's introduction by the Minister for the Arts of a three year grant-in-aid settlement. Provided these forward commitments prove realistic, they will greatly help the national museums in their planning.

We appreciate, too, the additional money the Minister for the Arts has secured for 1988–89. But discussion is needed, not so much on the level of funding which can be secured, as on the funding needed by the national museums in order to carry out their essential functions. This is sometimes called core-funding, but the term is not apt in this connection: it implies too small and variable a proportion of the total. We prefer to talk of *basic funding*, in the sense of an irreducible minimum. This is the funding of activities essential to the holding and housing of the national collections; displaying, securing, conserving and where appropriate adding to them; and using them for educational and scholarly purposes and for the widest public benefit. The funding of those activities is a residual responsibility of the Government. It is not one that the Government can properly seek to share with Trustees, still less transfer to them (and we return to this in the next chapter).

Since the Minister for the Arts is committed not to review the levels of grant-in-aid announced for the three years up to 1990–91, it may be unrealistic to expect any revision of funding levels to take effect until then; but the level for 1991–92 will be determined this year. We hope this process of determination will take account of the needs of each museum in terms of basic funding for running costs (based on complements determined after Government staff inspections, and including adequate provision for training (see Chapter 5), and documentation and conservation (see Chapter 6), for building maintenance and for acquisitions (see Chapter 6). The national museums, for their part, will know that, since the total money available is bound to be limited, the more their needs for running costs and building maintenance, the less will be available for acquisitions, and *vice versa*.

Public funding for national museums must also, however, include capital provision for gallery refurbishment and extensions. Judgements on needs and priorities here will need to be made with due regard to the circumstances of different museums: for example, the age, nature and condition of their buildings; what is involved in redesigning their displays, and how often this needs to be done (for example, a Science Museum display on computers needs modernising every few years as technology advances).

Once the annual level of basic funding was agreed, the Government could in theory translate it into endowment funding. This would involve the museum receiving a capital sum sufficient to provide income equivalent to annual funding, and undertaking in return never, in any circumstances, to seek further public funding. We doubt whether the Government would want to part with the large capital sums involved, and thereby lose its only effective sanction – that of withholding the museum's annual grant-in-aid. And, though all museums would welcome the assured income that endowment funding would provide, probably none could properly bind itself in this way, with all the risks of high inflation and pay levels.

The Future of Private Funding

An increasingly important source of revenue for many national museums is the money they earn, whether from publications, from catering, from their shop (the National Portrait Gallery has been particularly successful), or in some cases from admission charges. There is scope for some to do a good deal more.

The present climate of Government policy presents the national museums with new challenges and opportunities to seek other types of private funding – donations and business sponsorship. But these cannot, in the nature of things, be relied upon as regular sources. They are liable to dry up in hard times, or on change of policy. They are likely, in any case, to be received, not for financing recurrent general expenditure (such as cleaning galleries or paying warders), but for specific projects or capital schemes.

Indeed, as to *donations* – whether from charitable trusts, private individuals or public companies – it is clear to us that, in so far as potential donors realise that gifts will serve merely to relieve the Exchequer's responsibility, they will be reluctant to make publicly funded national museums the object of their generosity, except for particular projects.

There are two points on taxation that relate to donations, by individuals and companies respectively.

First, the Finance Act 1986 allowed individuals to offset charitable donations against tax through the payroll-giving scheme, with the employer's co-operation, and up to a limit of only £120 in a year. This is soon to be doubled, but even £240 is quite ineffective. A proper tax incentive is badly needed. There is plenty of potential for private patronage of the national museums: recent years have seen great munificence – by, for instance, the Sainsbury family and the Clore Foundation – on a scale comparable to that of the great benefactors of the past; but many more large private donations will not materialise without fiscal reform allowing them to be offset against tax.

15

Second, the same Finance Act allowed a company to offset charitable donations against tax, up to three per cent of its annual dividend. We understand that up to October 1987, under this admirable provision, companies in the United Kingdom actually obtained tax relief on only about £20m donated to all charities. They could, under the 1986 Act, obtain relief on donations totalling over £500m a year. Clearly the national museums, like others, have major opportunities here to attract tax-deductible donations that would help to finance recapitalisation schemes such as displays and gallery refurbishment.

As to *sponsorship*, the Minister for the Arts has said[1] that allocation of a proportion of the money for national museums' buildings will in future depend partly on 'the extent to which they can raise money from other sources'. We hope the word 'can' was used deliberately, for success should not be the only criterion; account will need to be taken of potential as well as of performance. Because a company's decision to sponsor an exhibition or gallery is a business decision, based primarily on the likely advertising benefit, there are in practice wide variations between different national museums' potential for securing sponsorship. In general, the potential is greater for art galleries than for scientific museums; and much greater in London than, for example, on Merseyside or in Northern Ireland.

Finally in the context of private funding, we have considered whether national museums might be empowered to borrow or raise money on the financial market (as those in Northern Ireland are, and as the Science Museum for one would like to be). We are well aware of how radical a change this would be, and of the implications, but we consider that in the context of plural funding such a method of raising money should not be ruled out. We recognise that the option ought to be available only in certain circumstances and with appropriate safeguards. For example, Trustees would have to be forbidden to mortgage their buildings or collections. And a national museum should be able to borrow only for a development generating enough income (eg admission charges at the National Railway Museum in York) to service and repay the loan.

Summary

The national museums make an outstanding contribution to the nation's cultural life. In this chapter we have argued that the Government has a clear responsibility for basic funding of their essential activities. Some are better placed than others to supplement this with private funding for development.

---

[1] House of Commons Official Report, 16 December 1987

4. Trusting the Trustees

The system of Trustees is central to national museum arrangements in this country. Yet the nature of the Trustees' role and the recent changes in it, the manner of their appointment, and the way in which the system actually works, are all matters which have received less discussion and consideration than they deserve. This chapter discusses them at some length, together with issues of Government control, and we believe it is not the least important in our report.

The Trustees' Role

In a national museum, it is the Trustees who own the collections and who have the statutory duty of caring for them and ensuring public access. In most cases they now maintain the buildings, too, and will soon own them. Yet, though the Trustees have the final responsibility, they have no executive role (it could hardly be otherwise, since they are unpaid and often have other commitments which preclude their devoting even one day a month to the museum). The Director is the Trustees' executive arm, and they should allow him or her to run the museum. Between them they should know enough to be sure it is being run in accordance with the policy and strategy they have approved, and that the collections are well used and cared for.

Appointment of Trustees

A glance at the Appendices will show that a high proportion of Trustees (about 80%) are appointed by Ministers. In some cases covered by modern legislation, the appointing Minister must have regard to the desirability of a Trustee having knowledge or experience which will be of use in the exercise of the Board's functions, but otherwise Ministers are not restricted in making appointments. In practice these are political only in the sense that they are made by Ministers. The Trustees' terms of appointment (generally five or seven years) reflect the expectation that they are not chosen for their support of any particular party.

The spectrum from which Trustees are appointed should be kept broad. And it is important that they should be appointed as individuals, for the personal contribution they can make, and not as mandated representatives of particular interests. Every Board of Trustees needs a mixture of people with different qualities and experience: some with influence in government and business circles, who may be able to help with funding issues; some who know about museums and understand how they work, who can put the work of the museum in perspective; and some who can spare the time to sit on committees and interview-boards, look at estimates, hear staff views, join in discussion of new activities. Ideally, all Trustees should have the time to enable them to become familiar with the museum. It will be ill served if too many of those appointed, whatever their qualities, cannot spare significant time for Trustee work. And, the more heavily committed some Trustees are, the more the need for others who can carry the burden of day-to-day work.

In some national museums the Chairman of the Trustees is appointed by the Minister (or Prime Minister); in others, the Chairman is chosen by the Trustees from among their number. We see advantages in each course, and no great merit in uniformity. What matters is recognition of the key importance of the Chairman's role, and of his or her essential independence. This is crucial, alike in the style the Chairman sets for a Board of Trustees, in day-to-day relations with the Director, and in external relations.

Before a Trustee is appointed, there is often – but not always, we believe – consultation with the Chairman of the Trustees. The Chairman knows the chemistry of the Board and the balance it needs; he should, we think, as a matter of prudence as well as of courtesy, always be consulted, both as to the sort of Trustee required and as to a person the Minister may have it in mind to appoint. And the Chairman's views, once sought, ought not lightly to be set aside.

Equally important is the information and briefing given to a new Trustee before appointment. At present, when someone is invited to become a Trustee of a museum, very little background information on it is given. In future, we think, the letter from the Minister's office should enclose information on how the museum is organised and run, the respective roles of the Trustees and the Director, and what a Trustee's duties will involve; and it should indicate any special qualities being looked for in filling the vacancy. It might also suggest that the Chairman of Trustees or the Director would be glad to meet the person being invited, and to discuss any issues he or she might wish to raise.

Some may feel that provision of this information to a future Trustee is unnecessary. Others may be surprised it is not provided already. We see it as an important token of the importance of Trustees' appointments, and of their having a proper basis for taking office.

Accountability

Once appointed, a Trustee may resign at any time. In the case of many national museums, there is no specific statutory provision for the appointment to be terminated. We think there should be (and the standard guidance on public bodies[1] says as much), on grounds of prolonged absence, bankruptcy, incapacity or unfitness for office.

Most Boards of Trustees are required to publish a report every three years. We think an annual report would be more in keeping with their accountability to Parliament and public. It need not be elaborate or expensive, and could accompany the annual accounts they are already required to provide. The funding Department[2] could ask for the report to include particular information (in relation, for example, to the corporate plan).

In the last resort, Trustees are answerable to the courts. Last year, in the case of a private Trust[3] owning a museum, the Attorney-General successfully moved the High Court for an order to replace the Trustees. Short of this, and of possible intervention by the Charity Commissioners, the Government's only sanction, if the Trustees saw fit to move out of line, would be to withhold, or threaten to withhold, all or part of the annual grant-in-aid, which would be largely self-defeating.

Arm's Length Control

In Government parlance, a national museum is a non-departmental public body. It operates at what has for many years been called arm's length from the Government, so that the Trustees may function free from day-to-day Government intervention based on short-term expediency. At the same time, it needs to be subject to certain controls to ensure that the public funds it receives are properly spent on the purposes for which they were voted by Parliament.

Clearly there is an inherent tension between these two positions. The Trustees will, reasonably or unreasonably, expect from the Government adequate funding, and freedom from interference. The Government will, reasonably or unreasonably, expect from the Trustees value for public money, and operation within the broad framework of Government policy, whether this be economic (for example, the level of grant-in-aid) or cultural (for example, the priority to be given to Scottish culture by the national museums in Edinburgh).

---

[1] Non-Departmental Public bodies: A Guide for Departments (HMSO, 1987)

[2] Because of possible confusion with business sponsorship, we avoid the term sponsoring or sponsor Department.

[3] The Trustees of the Henry Reitlinger Bequest, who own a museum in Maidenhead.

A study of the legislation throws no light on how this tension may be resolved. Section 4(6) of the National Galleries of Scotland Act 1906 placed a duty on the Trustees to comply with any instruction issued by the Secretary of State, but this was replaced in 1985 by provisions[1] containing no such duty. Again the National Heritage Act 1983 does not, in the case of the V & A and Science Museums, empower the Secretary of State to attach conditions to payment of grant. But it does do so in the case of the Royal Armouries. We instance these points, not to quibble, but to illustrate the uncertainty and imprecision surrounding the relationship between Government and Trustees, and the degree of control that is appropriate. No one questions the need for the Government to make the payment of grant-in-aid subject to financial control. The issues are what controls are necessary, and – no less important – how they are exercised.

A funding Department pays grant-in-aid on conditions set out in a Financial Memorandum. This is issued after consultation with the national museum, and takes a fairly standard form, based on Treasury guidance. The museum is required to submit annual estimates and forecasts; monitor payments and receipts, and report likely over- or under-spending; submit annual accounts; maintain systems of financial management and internal audit; report novel or contentious payments; report on the organisation and effect of financial control; and seek approval for new posts above a certain level.

These controls, backed up by periodic reports from the National Audit Office, are designed to enable the funding Department to satisfy itself that there has been no mismanagement in the spending of public money. Last year's report by the Public Accounts Committee[2] was critical of the National Museum of Wales for failing to secure economy and effectiveness in the use of public funds, and of the Welsh Office for failing to discharge properly its responsibilities as the funding Department. Inevitably this report and its background have coloured the view of the Treasury and of funding Departments, and indeed of national museums. Nevertheless, it has not been suggested that the substance of control on national museums is insufficient, and we ourselves would like to see a conscious and continuing effort to minimise that substance.

What concerns us at least as much as the substance of any necessary controls is how they are exercised, in what spirit, and with what object. The Public Accounts Committee's report addressed this point. A funding Department, it said, should clearly distinguish between policies, which are the responsibility of the museum itself, and the need for assurance about sound administrative and financial control systems for

[1] National Heritage (Scotland) Act 1985
[2] Fifteenth Report, Session 1986–87

expenditure of grant-in-aid. We agree. But we have observed that certain funding Departments seem reluctant to relinquish control of policy to the Trustees, and loath to give them that independence of function, discussion and decision which is properly theirs.

One example of this reluctance is the insistence on having an assessor at Trustees' meetings. Some Departments want their assessor to be present throughout every Trustees' meeting. We accept that the presence of assessors can be useful (though their role and influence depend on personalities), but we think they should attend only on the Trustees' invitation.

In the relationship between a national museum and its funding Department, there should be clear lines of demarcation, leading to mutual confidence and respect. The museum should accept the Department's duty in relation to financial control. The funding Department, for its part, should allow the Trustees to perform the role derived from their statutory duties. It should recognise that experienced and distinguished Trustees undertake this task as a form of unpaid public service. Except in fairly strict relation to financial control, they will hardly tolerate being told by a departmental official how to perform their task and order their priorities. Departments will do well to have this threshold of tolerance in mind when they carry out their financial management and policy reviews. The approach, moreover, should be reasonably uniform as between different Departments and parts of the United Kingdom. We are glad to note that the Treasury, in its response[1] to the Public Accounts Committee in October 1987, says it seeks to ensure a common approach on such matters.

The Future of Trustees

The role of Trustees has changed quite fundamentally in the last few years. They are no longer seen simply as dignified watchdogs. The perception of their role has become larger, the expectation greater, and their practical, legal and financial responsibilities broader. We have already noted their new responsibilities for museum buildings, and their increasing commercial preoccupation. Above all, as we observed in Chapter 3, they are faced with consistent underfunding and expected to become self-reliant.

Until recently, Trustees could look to the Government for the money they needed for essential funding. They did not always get all they wanted, but both they and the Government knew where funding responsibility lay. Now the Government is seeking to share this responsibility for essential funding with the Trustees by saying, in effect, that it is

[1] Cm 236

providing only so much, and the Trustees must find the balance. Indeed, we see the Government as possibly moving towards the position of saying that, while it will continue to contribute substantially for the time being, it is the Trustees who have the residual responsibility for the museum's funding. Such a position would not, in our view, be compatible with the system of unpaid Trustees. These Trustees give their valuable time in order to see that the museum is run well and the collections are well used and cared for. They accept appointment in the expectation of being given the means to achieve that end. To tell them they should be responsible for the means as well as the end would be to change the nature of their trusteeship.

Although the governing bodies of the national museums are having to function commercially to an extent, and may need more commercial freedom, they could never operate like the board of a limited company, with the freedom of say the Board of British Rail, since their receipt of grant-in-aid would necessitate continued financial control. It could be argued that their Chairman and members should be eligible for payment (as those of English Heritage and the British Library Board are) on the ground that payment would bring in people as Trustees who could not otherwise afford to serve. We do not in fact believe it would enhance their quality. And it would militate against the museums' best interests by blurring the clear and valuable distinction between unpaid Trustees and salaried staff.

We attach great importance to the tradition of voluntary service. Over the years, the Trustees' contribution has been invaluable and their independence unquestioned. Beyond doubt, the system of unpaid Trustees has served the national museums well, and we earnestly hope it will continue. But this must be subject to what we have said above about Trustees' appointments, accountability and control, and to their being adequately funded. In essence, Trustees must feel that they are trusted – and allowed – to discharge their trust. They must be enabled to see their unpaid public service as worthwhile, in the sense that its public funding is commensurate with the public duty they have undertaken.

Summary

In this chapter we have argued that, with certain changes we have indicated, the system of unpaid Trustees governing the national museums should continue; but it can do so only if committed Trustees see their task as worthwhile in terms of being given the freedom, and the means, to perform it sensibly. If this is not the case, suitable people will be unwilling to be appointed, and the system will be jeopardised.

5. National Museum Staff

General

The staff of national museums are not civil servants; but, by virtue of an agreement[1] made in 1964 between the Government and the staff organisations, they are treated as though they were. This is achieved in practice by requiring the Trustees to exercise certain of their functions subject to the Government's approval, which is given only if civil service rules and procedures are followed. So the writ of the Civil Service Commission runs in national museums, their staff have gradings comparable to those in the civil service, the Government pension scheme applies to them and – most importantly – their pay levels are effectively determined by the Government.

The main disadvantage of this arrangement is its inflexibility: on complementing (through staff inspections, often carried out by civil servants who know little of museum work); on gradings (which are subject to formal Treasury guidance); and on rates of pay (with some consequences that we noted in Chapter 3 and others that we note on page 25 below). On the other hand, it must be said that the staff like the tie with the civil service; they know where they stand. In theory it would help the national museums if the tie were broken. In practice this would probably create as many problems as it would solve. We advocate rather a loosening of the tie – of the sort that may in any case result from the changes within the civil service which we understand to be now under consideration.

Directors

National museum Directors are, inevitably, regarded as leaders of the museum profession. They may not be the only leaders, but it is on them that leadership falls. They are the Government's Expert Advisers in a number of contexts: on items offered in lieu of tax; on applications for government indemnity for items borrowed for temporary exhibition; on items referred to the Reviewing Committee on the Export of Works of Art. This function of Expert Adviser is one they exercise *ex officio*. They may delegate it to senior staff in particular cases, but the function is

---

[1] The so-called Couzens–Hayward Agreement.

theirs, and one to which they, as well as the Government, attach import-ance. It is, however, often extremely demanding in terms of time.

We referred in Chapter 4 to the respective roles of Trustees and Director. A good working relationship between the two is crucial to a museum's successful operation; but there can be no blueprint. It in-volves both a closeness and a distance, and there should be mutual confidence and understanding; but how that confidence and under-standing are reached will vary with the personalities involved and with the traditions of the museum.

The Director is appointed by the Trustees, subject to Government approval. The trend in recent years has been towards appointing Direc-tors on fixed-term contracts, and about half now hold office on this basis. The decision to offer appointment on a fixed-term contract should be for the Trustees to make, but the Government clearly favours this course because it allows for greater management flexibility and career mobility. In principle, we agree. In practice, we are concerned that it may in the longer term discourage people from applying for Director posts, and make it even harder than it is now to find enough good applicants. We think Trustees should be able to advertise and make the appointment on whichever basis they think right. At the same time, more flexibility is needed. If, for example, a Curator A is appointed Director on a fixed-term contract, he should on its completion be able to revert to pension-able service as Curator A. And those on permanent appointment should be able to retire early with compensation.

The gradings of the national museum Directors were reviewed in 1987. In line with the general trend in Whitehall, there now seem to be prospects of progress towards greater flexibility in fixing individual Directors' salaries.

There is frequent consultation between individual Directors. They also meet together at regular intervals in the Conference of National Directors. This body has no powers or formal standing, but it is poten-tially useful and could provide an effective means of co-ordination – for example in discussing this report and considering any joint action that may be required in consequence.

The national museums must continue to be headed by men and women of outstanding ability, and the Director's job must remain satis-fying and stimulating enough to attract the best people. This satisfaction is by no means self-evident, for the nature of the job has been changing in the last ten or twenty years: it has become more demanding, and the pressures are increasing. On the one hand, some Trustees have occa-sionally seemed unwilling to leave the professional running of the museum to the Director. On the other hand, Directors find themselves increasingly preoccupied with management, with problems of adminis-tration and finance, and with marketing and fund-raising. This is not a new problem. Nor is it simply a United Kingdom phenomenon: museum directors in the United States have the same experience. Nor indeed is it peculiar to museums (there are obvious parallels in universities).

The administration of a big national museum is nowadays extremely complex. But it needs more than administration: it needs leadership. In the end it is the Director who will provide the museum with his or her own vision, put a personal stamp on it, and largely determine its organisation and structure.

Two characteristics of museums generally have been the assumption that curatorial experts can turn into managers automatically on promotion, and the absence of any developed training or recognised specialism as museum administrator. Clearly, potential Directors should receive management training, as we say later in this chapter. And the appointment of a senior administrator may relieve the Director (though such a person should be sympathetic to the museum's curatorial work, which should not be seen as subordinated to administrative considerations). Above all, it is important that the Director should have a scholarly background, so as to be in a position to give scholarly direction to the museum's activities (and we are glad to note that recent appointments have taken this consideration into account).

Other Staff

Of some 12,000 people employed in United Kingdom museums, over half work in the national museums. Table 2 shows a 1987 total of 6,420 staff (with Merseyside, 18% more than ten years earlier; without, 8%). The Appendices show that 2,368 of these are warding staff, and 1,714 are curators and conservators.

Many of the curatorial staff are members of one of the civil service staff associations. Both the First Division Association (FDA) and the Institute of Professional Civil Servants (IPCS) have provided us with papers in connexion with this report, and we gratefully acknowledge their help. We were glad too, when we visited Belfast in March 1987, to meet representatives of the Northern Ireland Public Service Alliance. The main concern of all the staff organisations is the extent to which the national museums are underfunded by the Government, and the implications of this, in terms of the freezing of posts, the growing backlogs of work, and eventually the need to close galleries and even departments. Another concern, which we fully share, is the extent to which the shortfall in funding has caused priorities to be distorted, with commercial achievement often ranked higher than scholarship. If a national museum has to divert the efforts of its curatorial staff to the time-consuming task of fund-raising, it is living off its intellectual capital and jeopardising its future operation.

The national museums vary greatly in size: four have more than 500 staff, and four have fewer than 100. The largest can provide adequate career opportunities for their staff, and indeed many people do spend their whole working lives in one museum. We favour the principle of cross-fertilisation, though we recognise that it is practicable only in certain fields. More staff movement in and out would benefit both staff and museums. Staff of national museums succeed from time to time in applications for appointments in local museums. We should like to see the national museums advertising their middle- and senior-grade posts more often, and appearing more ready to appoint people from outside with different experience and new ideas. This would be good for the museum service as a whole.

With their staff tied to civil service grades and salaries, the national museums inevitably experience difficulty in recruiting to certain grades for which the private sector pays more. This is true, for example, of secretarial staff, and of design, scientific and certain other specialist staff. A Director cannot run a great museum shackled to pay-scales worked out for Whitehall, when these are unrelated to museum problems. Where they can show the need, national museums should be allowed some flexibility in rates of pay.

Few national museums have made much use of teams from the Manpower Services Commission which have done valuable work in many smaller museums. And in general they make relatively little use of volunteers. Some (such as the British Museum) use a few who possess a particular rare expertise. Some (such as the National Army Museum) use them in the shop. Many would like to use volunteers more, but all are conscious of their varying reliability, and of the time involved in their supervision. Not surprisingly, the staff organisations dislike the prospect of volunteers being used to conceal staff shortages.

Training

Throughout the museum profession, attitudes to staff training are being reassessed in the light of the Hale Report.[1] In the national museums, this reassessment may lead to a more systematic approach than is the case now. Certainly the staff organisations want to encourage better training. They say it has had low priority, and see this as a factor in undermining curatorial morale.

General curatorial training may not always be appropriate for all curatorial posts in national museums, but all their staff need a core of museum-oriented training; and those intending to apply for posts in

[1] Museum Professional Training and Career Structure: Report by a Working Party of the Museums & Galleries Commission (HMSO, 1987)

26

other museums will need full training. We believe it will be to the advantage of the national museums to participate in a nationally agreed training scheme such as the Hale Report proposed, and not to try to bypass or duplicate it.

Most national museums now have designated training officers, though not all these have detailed training experience. Some meet regularly as a group, and are devising training policies and instituting short specialised courses. We welcome these developments. We should like to see training officers designated at an appropriate level (say, Grade C), and the co-ordination of in-house training opportunities between national museums. The Hale Report recommended a full-time training officer, based in one of them, to undertake this task.

Of the curatorial and conservation staff who enter national museums at Grade G, many are graduates who are frustrated when they find themselves given no systematic training or encouragement to gain promotion. There seems to us a strong case for more flexible arrangements, allowing for graduate entry at various levels. Those who enter at Grade F should be required (as the Hale Report recommended) to gain the new Certificate in Museum Practice in this grade, and the new Advanced Certificate to progress to Grades E and D.

In the higher grades – Grade C and above – management training is now widely seen as essential. It should be a pre-requisite for promotion to Grade C (and for certain posts, such as head of security, in addition to specialist training). Several national museums already take advantage of management courses at the Civil Service College. This is to be encouraged: any potential future Director would do well to take such a course. The College itself has expressed interest in tailoring its courses to museum work if the demand develops, and there are other bodies (such as the Industrial Society) who might provide this training. For this reason the Hale Report did not think a separate staff college arrangement for the museum profession was desirable or necessary.

In principle, too, the national museums are well placed to offer training to staff of other museums. It is part of their educational role to be able to provide specialist courses in areas where they have particular expertise (for example, geological conservation, numismatics); to provide internships and scholarships (as, for example, the National Gallery and the Tate do now); to provide staff to participate in pre-entry training; to offer training in the specific context of travelling exhibitions. There is scope, too, for co-operation with educational institutions. For example, the V & A runs an MA degree course on the history of design with the Royal College of Art, and is to run one on conservation and restoration with Imperial College and the Royal College.

Moreover, as we observed at the end of Chapter 2, the movement need not always be in one direction. By means of exchanges and attachments, national museum staff could gain valuable experience of the non-national sector, offering specialist expertise in, for example, cataloguing important collections. Such exchanges are no doubt difficult to organise and staff cannot always be spared, but they are clearly of considerable potential value, and help to create mobility and a sense of unity within the museum profession.

Training is needed also for non-professional staff, particularly those who come into contact with the public. Most people visiting a museum never see a curator. Every visitor comes in contact with warding staff, and the quality of his or her experience is greatly influenced by their attitude. The national museums attract millions of overseas visitors every year. Yet tourist agencies have been critical of the way some of them treat their visitors, and of the attitude of some warders. Warding staff need initial and refresher training, not only in security, but in how to relate to visitors and make them feel welcome.

The general approach of Sir John Hale and his working party was to tailor training to individual needs: their proposed new training structure would cater for all staff, every role and specialism, and in every type of museum. This, they believed, would eliminate divisiveness between curators and other staff, and between national museums and others. We endorse this aim. We see training as a key means of integrating national museum staff in a united museum profession. It needs a higher priority within the national museums than it has now, and specifically the commitment of more staff and money.

Summary

In this chapter we have discussed important issues relating to the direction, organisation and staffing of national museums. A museum is as good as its collections, and as the people who run it. On their professionalism, their commitment and their morale will turn its success in promoting the public's understanding and enjoyment. To achieve this success, national museums need to give priority to investment in staff management and training.

6. Aspects of the Collections

In this chapter we discuss acquisitions, collecting policies and disposals; together with the key subjects of documentation, conservation and security.

Acquisitions

All the national museums, save the Wallace Collection (to which no additions are made) have an implied duty to augment their collections. Many have an explicit statutory duty[1] to add to (as well as care for and preserve) the objects in their collections. They need to be able to acquire items, small and great, that become available on the international market, for reasons that may be either general (to create knowledge, or broaden experience) or particular (to continue sequential collections, or fill gaps). In doing so they will generally be pursuing a careful collecting policy, related to the means at their disposal; though this policy is liable to be distorted periodically by the need to buy 'heritage' objects threatened with export.

In order to be able to make these acquisitions, national museums need purchase grants commensurate with current prices. We deplore the steady erosion of the purchasing power of these grants. To restore this purchasing power to the level of ten years ago should be the objective for the Minister for the Arts and his colleagues.

Here we pay tribute to the organisations that have helped national museums to make acquisitions, despite their meagre purchase grants, when opportunity has offered: the National Heritage Memorial Fund, which has used Government money with infinite resource and sagacity; the National Art-Collections Fund, foremost among art charities, which has contributed to many important purchases over the years; and the other trusts, private donors and friends' organisations that have helped with purchases at critical times.

Collecting Policies

With purchasing so problematical, it is all the more important that each national museum should have a clear, though not necessarily detailed, published collecting policy.

---

[1] The V & A Museum, for example, in section 2 of the National Heritage Act 1983.

We see the publication of collecting policies as part of the Trustees' accountability; and, beyond this, as helping to promote mutual understanding between museums. By exposing areas of overlap, they can be expected to stimulate dialogue, to discourage insularity and to encourage co-operation, rather than the reverse, between the national museums themselves and with other museums.

Overlaps and potential conflicts of interest between national and local museums can cause friction – as is the case, for example, with archaeological material. The publication of the national museums' collecting policies may clear the air here. This would be the more likely if, when publishing its policy, a national museum were to invite discussion, and indicate a willingness at least to consider modifying its policy in the light of representations.

We favour the national museums concerting their policies in appropriate cases, where significant public money can be saved or other clear advantage seen. From among numerous areas of overlap, we instance only two: first, the fact that the National Museums of Scotland and the National Galleries of Scotland both now collect European sculpture; second, the fact that the Science Museum, the Imperial War Museum and the Royal Air Force Museum all collect aircraft. In such areas of overlap, progress can probably best be made by the Directors getting together, perhaps with a small number of Trustees.

In some areas, particularly the newer collecting areas, action is being taken or has already been taken. We instance the agreement on sculpture-collecting by the V & A (up to 1920) and the Tate (after 1920); the National Maritime Museum's initiative on preserving historic ships; and the recent agreement between the National Gallery and the British Museum that the latter should start a national collection of icons.

Collecting policies of national museums need not, however, be exclusive. Not all overlaps are undesirable. Each instance deserves separate study. There are, for example, the obvious considerations of distance and ease of access, which may justify overlaps between, say, London and Merseyside, or Cardiff and Belfast. Then different museums collect for different reasons: one may collect primarily from the point of view of design, while another collects historically documented pieces. Again, overlap in certain areas may induce healthy competition between national museums (though not to the point of their bidding against each other at auction). Such competition obviously exists between London and, for example, Edinburgh and Cardiff.

There have been occasional advocates of wholesale rationalisation of some of the national museums' existing holdings (for example, by moving Constable paintings from the V & A to the Tate). We would not support such rationalisation as a cause, any more than we support the rigid exclusion of collecting overlaps. Even if, in a particular case, such an approach were arguably the best, it might well be the enemy of the good. Many of the present anomalies stem from generous bequests of varied collections to particular museums. And any long-term financial or scholarly advantages that rationalisation might bring would be liable to be outweighed by the upheaval, confusion and dissipation of curatorial effort it would involve.

What we do wish to see is the continuation of close co-operation between the national museums, the fostering of friendly relations between their staff, Directors and Trustees, and a general consciousness of their all serving the collective public interest. Recognising such a commonality of interest and purpose is more likely to produce sensible results than pursuing the chimera of rationalisation.

Disposals

Disposal is a process of which many museums make use from time to time, especially, for example, those which acquire contemporary objects. They must be able to weed periodically and discard when necessary. But, in the case of a national museum, this should be a free choice by the Trustees advised by the Director. Disposal should not be forced on them directly by the Government's urging them to 'manage' their collection, or indirectly by its failure to provide the basic funding the museum needs. In this connection we have consistently made two points.

First, we would expect any Trustees, given the power to dispose of items they consider unsuitable for retention in their collection, to use it with discrimination. Equally, we would not expect such a power to be conferred on Trustees indiscriminately, but only where it can be shown to be necessary and appropriate. In the case of the National Gallery Trustees in particular, this power is neither necessary nor appropriate (and the present Trustees do not seek or want it). The Trustees of the National Galleries of Scotland do have such a power, and may need it in relation especially to the Scottish National Gallery of Modern Art. Our view, which we have made clear to the Minister for the Arts, is that Parliament should not be asked to confer such a power on the National Gallery Trustees.

Second, the Commission's registration guidelines (broadly following the Museums Association's Code of Practice) indicate that, before any item is disposed of, it should first be offered to another registered museum by loan, exchange or gift. In general, a transfer or indefinite loan to another museum that might have a specialist interest is preferable to sale.

Documentation

The need for stocktaking of national museum collections, based on inventories and good documentation, was first urged by the Treasury as early as 1886, and has since been pursued by the Public Accounts Committee. In the last few years most national museums have been active in developing computerised systems and procedures, but progress has been slow and uneven. Not all have been able to find the money needed, or been able to justify setting up a documentation department or appointing a registrar responsible for documenting acquisitions and loans. These are important matters for the museums themselves.

Our chief concern is that, when considering what new systems and procedures to introduce, a national museum should not be insular, but should think (as we said in Chapter 2) in terms of the widest public benefit. The possibilities are enormous. There are opportunities for a museum to disseminate information about its collections; to allow direct access, by researchers and other museums in this country and overseas, to most categories of its collection information (eventually, no doubt, in return for having access to theirs); and to provide and market textual and visual information in machine-readable form. There are opportunities, too, for national and local museums to pool records and develop joint specialist databases (for example, an inventory of palaeontological type specimens).

To this end we are anxious to encourage the national museums to co-operate closely on such matters as developing common standards and terminologies, and to involve the Museum Documentation Association, which is well-placed to advise across the whole documentation field.

Conservation

Even more daunting than the problem of documentation is the need to arrest the inexorable process of deterioration; and the provision of correct display and storage conditions may well need to claim priority over conservation practice by way of active intervention. Indeed, if two performance indicators in the conservation field were needed, the first might be the proportion of the collections still held in adverse environmental conditions; and the second, the proportion in urgent need of conservation.

The larger national museums have long recognised the key importance of conservation, and made striking progress in recent years. Across the whole field of conservation practice, as well as in research on conservation processes and materials, and in scientific analytical research, they have given a lead by attaining and maintaining the highest professional standards. To take only one example, the annual National Gallery

Technical Bulletin, started in 1977, is now established as a journal of the highest international repute.

Several national museums already have separate departments of conservation, with their heads at broadly the level of keeper, and with their own budgets. The others will wish to consider adopting such an arrangement, on the grounds that it allows resources to be used to the best effect. It also facilitates greater co-operation between the national museums.

Regular meetings already take place between heads of conservation and heads of research where these posts exist. A more general co-operative framework would allow for work to be distributed, purchase of equipment concerted, facilities shared, samples exchanged and research programmes correlated. We see scope, too, for more work with universities; this could provide access to a wider range of expertise and facilities. Greater use could be made, too, of collaborative research schemes under the aegis of the Science and Engineering Research Council.

A practical form of collaboration is the sharing of expertise where one national museum specialises in the conservation of some material. An example is the British Museum's seconding a paper conservator to work on the Leonardo cartoon at the National Gallery.

In Chapter 2 we identified two duties of a national museum as being to excel in scholarship, and to ensure the widest possible benefit from its collections and the learning based upon them. So it is with conservation, where the national museums have a vital educational role to play. It would be helpful if smaller museums could send more of their conservators to the national museums for short visits, attachments, occasional exchanges, vacation secondments during training courses, and internships for newly trained conservators. Not only would individual staff benefit; the museum community as a whole would benefit from this extension of the corpus of conservation knowledge and experience.

Thus we have dwelt on the leading conservation role played by the larger national museums, and on the need to make the best use of resources – in terms of internal organisation, and in terms of further co-operation between national museums and with other museums.

Security

In all national museums, security remains a serious and expensive preoccupation. For professional advice on the organisation, deployment and oversight of their warding staff they look to the National Museums Security Adviser (a former senior police officer), who since 1981 has been a member of the Commission's staff. The creation of this post has proved of considerable value and importance to museums.

The Security Adviser advises on all aspects of security: he visits by invitation to discuss security systems for new, refurbished and existing buildings, takes part in reviews of the number and deployment of warding staff, and follows up any thefts; oversees the running of training courses for warding staff, gives lectures, and meets security officers quarterly; inspects the receiving museum's premises when items are to be lent from a national collection, or when items are accepted in lieu of tax; maintains records of the security arrangements at foreign institutions to which items are lent, and visits the locations of major touring exhibitions. He also gives *ad hoc* advice to non-national museums on security matters, and maintains contact with police forces at home and abroad.

The Security Adviser's contact in a national museum is the Director, who is ultimately responsible for its security, or the head of security acting on his behalf. In some national museums, the head of security is a full-time post. In others, the duties are performed by someone with other responsibilities – as accommodation officer, administrator or keeper – which may involve a conflict of interest. We endorse the Security Adviser's view that in a national museum this should be a full-time post. Only thus will the head of security have time for regular reviews of security arrangements, and be able to ensure a proper return from the museum's investment in warding staff. He will also be able to see to the supervision and training of warders, including the point about relations with visitors that we made in Chapter 5.

The shotgun attack on the Leonardo cartoon at the National Gallery last July led to some press questioning of the security arrangements in national museums. In any balance between protecting pictures and providing public access, the response must relate to the threat. In the last ten years, five paintings in national museums have suffered serious damage. All five attackers were detained; three were found to be in need of psychiatric care. The implements (one was a bunch of keys) used by four would not have been revealed by a bag search. The national museums' policy is to deploy uniformed attendants in galleries, with a search when there are indications that this is necessary. This is a flexible response which, in the National Museums Security Adviser's view, accords with the level of threat.

Postscript

The issues we have discussed in this chapter are those which, together with the important question of storage, form the subject of a report by the National Audit Office (NAO), published as our report was going to press. This was the NAO report on the Management of the Collections of the English National Museums and Galleries, which concentrated on the British Museum, the V & A and the Tate: the conservation and storage difficulties they face, and the risks involved for their collections.

These are difficulties we have seen for ourselves, on our visits to these and other national museums. The NAO report concluded by urging the need for priorities to be set and action planned to deal with these problems, acknowledging that this would take substantial resources, with no guarantee that adequate funds would be available. We were aware that the NAO report was in course of preparation, and that it would to some extent complement our own. The two reports should be considered together: issues of good housekeeping need to be addressed in the context of what we say (summarised in the next and final chapter) about the fundamental duties of the national museums, and their funding.

7. Conclusions

In this last chapter we restate our main conclusions. This is above all, as we said at the outset, a report of ideas and principles. It contains no list of numbered recommendations. We believe that, as a whole, it will be seen as a constructive contribution to the general debate on the national museums. And we shall be glad to join in discussing the issues we have raised.

National Museums Distinguished (Chapter 2)

The national museums are a magnificent inheritance held in trust for the future; they are a national and international asset of unrivalled quality, and also a significant economic asset. A national museum, we say, has a distinctive duty not only to care for and display its collections, but also to advance learning by means of research and scholarship based upon them; this is fundamental, and in the face of commercial pressures must be reasserted as a priority. A national museum has also a duty to promote public understanding and enjoyment, and to do so for the widest public by such means as loans and travelling exhibitions and exchanges with other museums.

Their Funding (Chapter 3)

Government funding of the national museums has increased significantly over the last ten years, as their activities have grown. But it has not been enough to cover their staff costs. A funding gap has thus been created, which has led to a curtailment of many museums' scholarly work, and to a decline in their educational and other services to the public. The value of purchase grants has declined by almost half in the last ten years, and their purchasing power needs to be restored. Most national museums have only recently been given responsibility for their buildings, and extra money will need to be provided if surveys show this to be required. We say that the Government has a responsibility to provide basic funding for a museum's essential activities – operating, purchase grant and buildings – based on approved staff complements, and should live up to this responsibility. The Government rightly encourages private funding for development (and certainly neither donations nor sponsorship can be relied on to meet recurrent expenditure). But not all the money needed for development can be expected from the private sector. In any case, the potential for attracting sponsorship varies widely between the national museums, and incentive-funding schemes must take this into account. A tax change is needed in order to stimulate private donations.

Their Trustees (Chapter 4)

We have reviewed the system of Trustees on which the national museums depend, and have found it to work well. We have suggested several improvements. Trustees should continue to be drawn from a broad spectrum, and should be properly briefed before appointment. Boards of Trustees should report every year as part of their accountability. The constitutional arm's length distance should be respected, and the aim should be the minimum of Government control. On this basis, we conclude, the system of unpaid Trustees can and should continue, provided that Trustees are given the means and the freedom to discharge their trust. It is unreasonable to make them responsible for raising money to meet the museum's basic needs. If Trustees do not see their unpaid public duty as worthwhile, in terms of the museum receiving commensurate funding, suitable people will be unwilling to serve.

Their Staff (Chapter 5)

Directors of national museums are the government's expert advisers in their fields. In order to be in a position to give direction to the museum's activities, they need to have a scholarly background. There should be more flexibility in their pay and conditions, and in those of other national museum staff. We call for more cross-fertilisation with local museums, and greater emphasis on training: participation in a nationally agreed training scheme, more management training, more training attachments, better training in dealing with visitors, more co-ordination of training opportunities; and generally more investment in staff management.

Their Collections (Chapter 6)

We say that overlaps in collecting policies are not necessarily undesirable, but that national museums should concert these policies where this could save significant public money. Nor do we advocate the rationalisation of their existing holdings; rather, we say, they should continue to co-operate in serving the collective public interest. We urge that Trustees should not be given disposal powers they do not want; they should not be pressed – directly, or indirectly through inadequate funding – to sell objects from their collections; they should rather give or lend them to another museum. We stress the importance of conservation, in terms of both priority and organisation, and of a systematic approach to documentation; and urge the need for national museums to co-operate with each other and with local museums in both these fields. We say that the national museums' flexible response to the security threat is right.

Their Achievement

Finally we want to draw together some of the ideas we have put forward, and to propose a basis on which a national museum's achievements may be judged, especially by Ministers of funding Departments.

The Trustees of a national museum are custodians of the principles underlying its existence. These involve at least three overriding obligations: first, to care for and display its collections, and advance learning by research and scholarship based upon them; second, to present its collections so that the public may understand and enjoy them; and third, to exercise leadership among museums by influence, help and example.

We believe that decisions on funding should be geared to a national museum's attaining objectives related to these obligations. And we see the first and third as keys to the second. Scholarly museum values must inspire and infuse every museum enterprise, whether it be mounting a travelling exhibition; instituting an educational programme; preparing a catalogue for sale; or devising a sponsored new display with interpretative material for visitors. In the long run, it is the museum's intrinsic quality that will attract visitors and sponsors alike. Commercial success should be seen to derive ultimately from museum values, and not *vice versa*.

Funding Departments rightly seek ways of judging a national museum's performance and achievement in return for public money. But performance indicators should relate not just to success in easily quantifiable areas, such as marketing and attracting visitors or sponsorship. They should relate first and foremost to qualitative museum values, in such activities as conservation, training, documentation, original scholarship and publications, and educational services in and outside the museum.

The national museums are great institutions, with much to be proud of. We are confident that they will continue to give a lead to the museum world by virtue of their excellence.

> 'Ah, but a man's reach should exceed his grasp,
> Or what's a heaven for?'
> *Browning: Andrea Del Sarto*

Notes on Tables and Appendices

1 Information in Tables 1–5 and the Appendices is derived from the museums themselves and their funding Departments. They have seen the material in draft, and every effort has been made to ensure accuracy. But, as in other aspects of museum activity, reliable statistics are notoriously hard to come by. The Commission has put in hand a study of how definitive basic museum statistics might best be compiled and made available.

2 In the Tables, the figures for the British Museum (Natural History) prior to 1985 are those for the Museum and the Geological Museum combined, before they amalgamated.

3 In the Tables, the figures for the National Museums of Scotland prior to 1985 are those for the Royal Scottish Museum and the National Museum of Antiquities of Scotland combined, before they amalgamated as the National Museums of Scotland.

4 In Tables 1–6 National Museums & Galleries on Merseyside is abbreviated as NMGM and appears as number 7 in the list of museums.

5 In Table 1 and the Appendices, attendance figures include those for satellite and branch museums except where otherwise indicated.

6 In Table 2 and the Appendices, two part-time staff are counted as one full-time; half figures are rounded up.

7 In Tables 3, 4 and 5, the Museums & Galleries Commission is abbreviated as the MGC.

8 In the Appendices, the date of foundation is the year of foundation of the oldest component institution.

9 In the Appendices, where a standard admission charge for adults is shown, this is for entry to the museum itself. In addition, and at some museums where entry is free, a separate charge is made for admission to certain exhibitions.

Table 1 **Attendance Figures**[a]

thousands

	1978	1979	1980	1981	1982	1983	1984	1985	1986	1987
1 British Museum	4,034	4,100	3,880	2,869	2,966	3,079	3,467	4,142	3,897	4,008
2 British Museum (Natural History)	2,901	2,869	2,410	2,807	2,444	2,663	3,022	3,354	3,240	1,633
3 Imperial War Museum	1,462	1,419	1,449	1,110	1,180	1,256	1,366	1,291	1,176	1,185
4 National Army Museum	72	69	72	63	49	65	65	91	75	84
5 National Gallery	2,300	2,758	2,618	2,738	2,633	2,897	2,937	3,157	3,182	3,567
6 National Maritime Museum	1,260	1,102	1,145	997	998	600	600	600	380	442
7 NMGM	—	—	—	—	—	600	—	—	1,163	1,329
8 National Portrait Gallery	400	400	400	500	524	468	581	516	625	591
9 Royal Air Force Museum	482	608	454	386	387	495	428	358	323	317
10 Royal Armouries	2,614	2,392	2,188	1,817	1,648	1,898	2,037	2,115	1,775	1,985
11 Science Museum	5,176	5,147	5,790	5,393	4,554	4,784	4,510	4,607	4,825	4,733
12 Tate Gallery	1,081	1,141	1,331	895	1,230	1,283	1,278	996	1,153	1,742
13 Victoria & Albert Museum	1,937	1,992	1,724	1,711	2,058	2,221	2,079	2,067	1,431	1,399
14 Wallace Collection	145	128	160	139	142	177	178	179	171	168
15 National Galleries of Scotland	388	442	421	437	426	442	469	538	530	524
16 National Museums of Scotland	700	744	768	721	730	765	724	751	701	817[b]
17 National Museum of Wales	700	700	700	700	700	700	800	800	800	1,039
18 Ulster Folk & Transport Museum	163	151	159	138	127	127	167	149	147	194
19 Ulster Museum	214	195	227	209	201	271	255	291	318	277
TOTAL	26,038	26,357	25,896	23,630	22,997	24,191	24,963	26,002	25,912	25,734

[a]Including branch museum attendance (Tate Gallery from 1981 onwards). [b]Includes the Scottish United Services Museum for the first time.

Table 2 **Numbers of Staff in Post**[a]

	~~96~~	1.4.74	1.4.77	~~80~~ 1.4.84	1.4.87	
1 British Museum	*1079*	931	969	1,008	1,005	*74 7.9*
2 British Museum (Natural History)		791	749	768	784	*− 7 −1*
3 Imperial War Museum		207	271	366	347	*140 68%*
4 National Army Museum		43	63	74	70	*27*
5 National Gallery		215	254	275	264	*49 22.8*
6 National Maritime Museum		207	315	409	333	*126 61%*
7 NMGM		—	—	—	551	
8 National Portrait Gallery		89	97	105	105	*16 17%*
9 Royal Air Force Museum		86	90	106	103	*17*
10 Royal Armouries		47	59	77	109	*62 128%*
11 Science Museum	*718*	430	520 *500*	474	587	*157 36.5*
12 Tate Gallery *336 (412) '94*		224	240	304	326	*102 456*
13 Victoria & Albert Museum *787*		646	670 *624*	667	665	*19 3 9*
14 Wallace Collection		68	72	77	76	*8 11*
15 National Galleries of Scotland		108	122 *135½*	127	127	*19*
16 National Museums of Scotland		237	247	233	247	*10*
17 National Museum of Wales		293	387	407	416	*123*
18 Ulster Folk & Transport Museum		137	150	145	148	*11*
19 Ulster Museum		132	147	155	157	*25*
TOTAL		4,891	5,422	5,777	6,420	

[a]Including staff at branch museums.

Table 3 Government Grants – Running Costs[a]

£ thousand cash

	1979–80	1980–81	1981–82	1982–83	1983–84	1984–85	1985–86	1986–87	1987–88[b]	1988–89[c]
1 British Museum	6,802	8,624	9,441	10,012	10,733	11,034	11,593	11,945	12,538	15,665[g]
2 British Museum (Natural History)	5,725	7,307	8,336	8,880	9,235	9,541	11,225	11,597	12,168	15,370[g]
3 Imperial War Museum	2,375	3,017	3,599	3,784	3,900	3,953	4,345	4,397	4,627	6,318[g]
4 National Army Museum	543	574	755	956	929	1,220	1,331	1,414	1,476	1,546
5 National Gallery	1,829	2,436	2,727	3,017	3,328	3,661	3,821	4,021	4,267	5,233[g]
6 National Maritime Museum	2,384	3,137	3,385	3,614	3,785	4,072	4,013	4,257	4,472	5,530[g]
7 NMGM[f]	—	—	—	—	—	—	—	9,395	8,664	9,470[g]
8 National Portrait Gallery	952	1,183	1,279	1,396	1,447	1,556	1,467	1,504	1,589	1,996[g]
9 Royal Air Force Museum	676[c]	732[c]	905[c]	1,044[c]	1,456[c]	1,472[c]	1,912	1,896	1,897	1,697
10 Royal Armouries	610[c]	758[c]	820[c]	895	1,260	2,140	2,467	2,390	2,490	2,504
11 Science Museum[d]	4,292	5,412	5,876	6,631	7,040	7,899	8,525	8,796	9,214	11,047[g]
12 Tate Gallery	2,067	3,396	2,887	3,163	3,299	3,553	3,829	3,967	4,682	6,300[g]
13 Victoria & Albert Museum[d]	4,584	6,040	6,589	7,181	7,865	8,906	9,525	9,878	10,535	12,900[g]
14 Wallace Collection	414	617	656	759	781	822	876	906	939	1,149[g]
15 National Galleries of Scotland	829	1,166	1,281	1,403	1,399	1,559	1,603	1,681	1,862	2,306[g]
16 National Museums of Scotland	1,643	2,164	2,382	2,462	2,577	2,872	3,100	3,940	4,232	5,226[g]
17 National Museum of Wales	3,244	4,017	4,553	4,882	5,122	5,634	6,061	6,419	5,661	5,803
18 Ulster Folk & Transport Museum[f]	1,608	1,631	1,456	1,455	1,497	1,479	1,709	1,862	1,814	1,846
19 Ulster Museum[f]	1,150	1,421	1,650	1,745	1,800	1,897	2,027	2,108	2,247	2,291
TOTAL	41,727	53,632	58,577	63,279	67,453	73,270	79,429	92,373	95,374	114,197

[a]Outturn expenditure, except where indicated. [b]Forecast outturn. [c]Provision.
[d]Excludes local museum purchase grants, paid to the Science Museum until 1985–86, and to the V & A until 1984–85, and to the MGC thereafter.
[e]Notional figure. [f]Includes funding for buildings.
[g]Includes additional funding for responsibilities (superannuation contributions, legal advice etc) previously borne on central departments' votes.

Table 4 Government Grants – Purchase Grants[a]

£ thousand cash

	1979–80	1980–81	1981–82	1982–83	1983–84	1984–85	1985–86	1986–87	1987–88[b]	1988–89[c]
1 British Museum	1,217	1,422	1,450	1,617	1,617	1,400	1,400	1,400	1,400	1,400
2 British Museum (Natural History)	87	113	157	171	181	190	190	190	190	190
3 Imperial War Museum	70	90	85	87	97	97	100	100	100	100
4 National Army Museum	50	70	70	80	90	95	100	105	109	109
5 National Gallery	2,612	3,109	2,930	2,988	3,331	3,331	2,750	2,750	2,750	2,750
6 National Maritime Museum	154	184	178	182	203	203	205	205	205	205
7 NMGM	—	—	—	—	—	—	—	750	750	750
8 National Portrait Gallery	244	291	272	278	310	310	310	310	310	310
9 Royal Air Force Museum	30	60	60	70	90	95	100	104	109	59
10 Royal Armouries	172	104	144	157	167	200	375[c]	283[c]	352	295
11 Science Museum[d]	104	300	329	336	374	374	375	375	375	375
12 Tate Gallery	1,570	1,888	1,794	1,830	2,041	2,041	1,815	1,815	1,815	1,815
13 Victoria & Albert Museum[d]	950	1,130	1,160	1,184	1,320	1,320	1,145	1,145	1,145	1,145
14 Wallace Collection	—	—	—	—	—	—	—	—	—	—
15 National Galleries of Scotland	685	897	941	1,211	1,265	1,274	1,439	1,517	1,555	1,578
16 National Museums of Scotland	277	360	382	495	520	524	591	503	560	642
17 National Museum of Wales	598	778	877	955	1,014	1,065	1,108	1,141	1,170	1,199
18 Ulster Folk & Transport Museum	16	—	—	—	—	20	25	55	71	87
19 Ulster Museum	150	—	—	—	—	30	45	135	136	167
TOTAL	8,986	10,796	10,829	11,641	12,620	12,569	12,073	12,883	13,102	13,176

[a]Outturn expenditure (excluding revotes), except where indicated. [b]Forecast outturn. [c]Provision.
[d]Excludes local museum purchase grants, paid to the Science Museum until 1985–86, and to the V & A until 1984–85, and to the MGC thereafter.

43

Table 5 **Government Grants – Total**[a]

£ thousand cash

	1979–80	1980–81	1981–82	1982–83	1983–84	1984–85	1985–86	1986–87	1987–88[b]	1988–89[c]
1 British Museum	8,019	10,046	10,891	11,629	12,350	12,434	12,993	13,345	13,938	**24,645**[f]
2 British Museum (Natural History)	5,812	7,420	8,493	9,051	9,416	9,731	11,415	11,787	17,858[f]	22,300[f]
3 Imperial War Museum	2,445	4,107	3,684	3,871	3,997	4,050	4,445	4,497	4,727	**12,938**[f]
4 National Army Museum	593[f]	644[f]	825[f]	1,036[f]	1,019[f]	1,315[f]	1,431[f]	1,519[f]	1,585[f]	1,655[f]
5 National Gallery	4,441	5,545	5,657	6,005	6,659	6,992	6,571	6,771	7,017	**11,473**[f]
6 National Maritime Museum	2,538	3,321	3,563	3,796	3,988	4,275	4,218	4,462	4,677	**8,245**[f]
7 NMGM						—	—	10,145[f]	9,414[f]	10,220[f]
8 National Portrait Gallery	1,196	1,474	1,551	1,674	1,757	1,866	1,777	1,814	1,899	**5,362**[f]
9 Royal Air Force Museum	706	792	965	1,114	1,546	1,567	2,012	2,000	2,006	1,756
10 Royal Armouries	782[e]	862[e]	964[e]	1,052	1,427	2,340	2,842	2,673	2,842	3,300[f]
11 Science Museum[d]	4,396	5,712	6,205	6,967	7,414	8,273	8,900	9,171	9,589	**16,632**[f]
12 Tate Gallery	3,637	5,284	4,681	4,993	5,340	5,594	5,644	5,782	6,497	**10,895**[f]
13 Victoria & Albert Museum[d]	5,534	7,170	7,749	8,365	9,185	10,226	10,670	11,023	11,680	**21,525**[f]
14 Wallace Collection	414	617	656	759	781	822	876	906	939	**1,598**[f]
15 National Galleries of Scotland	1,574	2,063	2,222	2,614	2,664	2,833	3,042	3,198	3,417	3,884
16 National Museums of Scotland	1,920	2,524	2,764	2,957	3,097	3,396	3,691	4,443	4,792	5,868
17 National Museum of Wales	3,842[f]	4,795[f]	5,430[f]	5,837[f]	6,136[f]	6,699[f]	7,169[f]	7,560[f]	6,831[f]	10,999[f]
18 Ulster Folk & Transport Museum	1,624[f]	1,631[f]	1,456[f]	1,455[f]	1,497[f]	1,499[f]	1,734[f]	1,917[f]	1,885[f]	1,939[f]
19 Ulster Museum	1,300[f]	1,421[f]	1,650[f]	1,745[f]	1,800[f]	1,927[f]	2,072[f]	2,243[f]	2,383[f]	2,640[f]
TOTAL	50,713	65,428	69,496	74,920	80,073	85,839	91,502	105,256	113,976	177,838[g]

[a] Outturn expenditure, excluding revotes, except where indicated.   [b] Forecast outturn.   [c] Provision.
[d] Excludes local museum purchase grants, paid to the Science Museum until 1985–86, and to the V & A until 1984–85, and to the MGC thereafter.
[e] Notional figure.   [f] Includes funding for buildings.
[g] The significant increase in this total, compared with the total for 1987–88, is due to the fact that the figures (**printed in bold**) for grant-in-aid to certain museums include for the first time provision for buildings, as detailed in the Appendices. See also Note[g] on Table 3.

Table 6 **National Heritage Memorial Fund Grants**

£ thousand cash

	1980–81	1981–82	1982–83	1983–84	1984–85	1985–86	1986–87
1 British Museum	—	215	250	—	613.2	100	1,005.5
2 British Museum (Natural History)	—	—	—	—	—	—	—
3 Imperial War Museum	—	—	14	28.7	—	—	198
4 National Army Museum	—	—	—	—	50	—	—
5 National Gallery	825	500	200	800	400	—	—
6 National Maritime Museum	—	30	63	25	76	28.8	250
7 NMGM	—	—	—	—	—	—	103.4
8 National Portrait Gallery	—	—	—	—	334	933	177
9 Royal Air Force Museum	—	—	—	32	—	—	—
10 Royal Armouries	—	—	—	186.5	—	94	25
11 Science Museum	—	111.5	—	32.5	20	20	50
12 Tate Gallery	—	—	150	45	50	—	—
13 Victoria & Albert Museum	40	460	22.3	135	55	20	465
14 Wallace Collection	—	—	—	—	—	—	—
15 National Galleries of Scotland	73	—	150	—	1,002	143	1,365
16 National Museums of Scotland	—	10	—	—	31	—	465
17 National Museum of Wales	—	—	20	—	15	—	41
18 Ulster Folk & Transport Museum	—	53	—	—	9	4.5	25
19 Ulster Museum	—	—	—	17	5	5	25
TOTAL NHMF GRANTS TO NATIONAL MUSEUMS	938	1,379.5	869.3	1,301.7	2,660.2	1,348.3	4,160.9

Appendix A **British Museum**

A major research institution, the museum also houses the national collections of art and archaeology from prehistoric time to the 20th century. It is divided into nine departments illustrating the breadth of human achievement: Egyptian, Greek and Roman, Oriental, Western Asiatic, Pre-historic and Romano-British, Medieval and Later Antiquities; and coins and medals, prints and drawings.

Date founded:	1753

Funding Department:	Office of Arts & Libraries

Governing Body:	Board of Trustees (25), appointed by the Sovereign (1), Prime Minister (14), Trustees (6), Others (4)

Authority:	British Museum Act 1963

Staff Numbers as at 1.4.87:		*Complement*	*In Post*
	Curatorial	297	268
	Warders	397	377
	Others	400	360
	TOTAL	1094	1005

		£
Grant-in-aid in 1988–89:	Running Costs	15,665,000
	Buildings	7,580,000
	Purchase Grant	1,400,000
	TOTAL	24,645,000

Attendance Figures (including branch museum) in 1987:	4,008,000

Main Building:	*Admission Charge*
Great Russell Street, London	None
Branch Museum:	
The Museum of Mankind, Burlington Gardens, London	None

Appendix B British Museum (Natural History)

The Museum has two functions: one as a scientific institution with national and international obligations for taxonomic and associated research based on its libraries and collections of natural history specimens; the other, a responsibility for education through its displays, teaching services and more popular publications.

Date founded:	1881

Funding Department:	Office of Arts & Libraries (since 1 August 1987)

Governing Body:	Board of Trustees (12), appointed by the Prime Minister (8), Trustees (3), Others (1)

Authority:	British Museum Act 1963

Staff Numbers as at 1.4.87:		*Complement*	*In Post*
	Curatorial	346	344
	Warders	142	138
	Others	345	302
	TOTAL	833	784

		£
Grant-in-aid in 1988–89:	Running Costs	15,370,000
	Buildings	6,740,000
	Purchase Grant	190,000
	TOTAL	22,300,000

Attendance Figures (including branch museum) in 1987:	1,633,092

Main Buildings: *Standard Admission Charge for Adults*

Natural History Museum, Cromwell Road, London	⎱ £2
Geological Museum, Cromwell Road, London	⎰

Branch Museum:

Zoological Museum, Tring	£1

Appendix C **Imperial War Museum**

The collections are devoted to all aspects of armed conflicts involving Britain and the Commonwealth since 1914. Exhibitions employ tableaux, documents, works of art and videos to depict the history of the two world wars and post war conflicts. The Museum's collections of 20th century film, sound recordings, documents, books, photography and works of art can be viewed by appointment.

Date founded:	1917

Funding Department:	Office of Arts & Libraries

Governing Body:	Board of Trustees (20), appointed by the Sovereign (1), Ministers (14), Commonwealth Governments (5)

Authority:	Imperial War Museum Act 1920

Staff Numbers as at 1.4.87:		*Complement*	*In Post*
	Curatorial	100	91
	Warders	145	142
	Others	118	114
	TOTAL	363	347

		£
Grant-in-aid in 1988–89:	Running Costs	6,318,000
	Buildings	6,520,000
	Purchase Grant	100,000
	TOTAL	12,938,000

Attendance Figures (including branch museums) in 1987:	1,184,959

Main Building:	*Standard Admission Charge for Adults*
Lambeth Road, London	None
Branch Museums:	
Cabinet War Rooms, London	£2.80
HMS Belfast, London	£3.00
Duxford Airfield	£3.50 (winter, £1)

48

Appendix D National Army Museum

The only United Kingdom museum focussing on the Army during its five centuries of existence. Two galleries chronologically survey this development: the Uniform Gallery, also displaying weaponry and medals, and the Art Gallery, which contains a comprehensive collection of 17th, 18th and 19th century portraiture and military paintings.

Date founded:	1960

Funding Department:	Ministry of Defence

Governing Body:	Council (12), appointed by the Army Board

Authority:	Royal Charter of 1971, as amended in 1984

Staff Numbers as at 1.4.87:		*Complement*	*In Post*
	Curatorial	29	33
	Warders	26	25
	Others	13	12
	TOTAL	68	70

		£
Grant-in-aid in 1988–89:	Running Costs	1,383,000
	Buildings	163,000
	Purchase Grant	109,000
	TOTAL	1,655,000

Attendance Figures (including branch museum) in 1987:	84,365

	Admission Charge
Main Building: Royal Hospital Road, London	None
Branch Museum: Sandhurst	None

49

Appendix E **National Gallery**

The national collection of painting, covering the major European schools up to 1900. Its entire collection of over 2,000 paintings is on permanent display.

Date founded:	1824
Funding Department:	Office of Arts & Libraries
Governing Body:	Board of Trustees (12), appointed by the Prime Minister (11), Tate Gallery (1)
Authority:	National Gallery and Tate Gallery Act 1954

Staff Numbers as at 1.4.87:

		Complement	*In Post*
	Curatorial	23	23
	Warders	202	181
	Others	70	60
	TOTAL	295	264

Grant-in-aid in 1988–89:

		£
	Running Costs	5,233,000
	Buildings	3,490,000
	Purchase Grant	2,750,000
	TOTAL	11,473,000

Attendance Figures in 1987: 3,566,568

Main Building: *Admission Charge*
Trafalgar Square, London   None

Appendix F National Maritime Museum

The Museum illustrates Britain's maritime history through its pre-eminent collection of nautical artefacts. Exhibits include shipmodels and boats, astronomical and navigational instruments, uniforms and weaponry, paintings and prints. It also houses a major library and archive, and is responsible for the Old Royal Observatory.

Date founded:	1934
Funding Department:	Office of Arts & Libraries
Governing Body:	Board of Trustees (12), appointed by the Prime Minister
Authority:	National Maritime Museum Act 1934

Staff Numbers as at 1.4.87:		*Complement*	*In Post*
	Curatorial	118	122
	Warders	120	127
	Others	76	84
	TOTAL	314	333

			£
Grant-in-aid in 1988–89:	Running Costs		5,530,000
	Buildings		2,510,000
	Purchase Grant		205,000
	TOTAL		8,245,000

Attendance Figures (excluding branch museums) in 1987:	442,055

Main Building:	*Standard Admission Charge for Adults*
Greenwich, London	
Old Royal Observatory, Greenwich	£2.20

Branch Museums:	
British Fisheries Museum, Brixham, Devon	30p
Cotehele Quay, St Dominick, Cornwall	20p
Herschel House and Museum, Bath	£1
Valhalla Museum, Tresco, Isles of Scilly	£2.50 (winter, £1)

Appendix G National Museums & Galleries on Merseyside

This complex comprises seven museums and galleries and a store open to the public. Together they are devoted to displaying the social, industrial and maritime history of Merseyside. Other collections include natural history, science, decorative arts, British and European painting and sculpture from 1400 to the present day.

Date founded:	1851 (Liverpool Museum), 1986 (as national museum)
Funding Department:	Office of Arts & Libraries
Governing Body:	Board of Trustees (14–20), appointed by the Chancellor of the Duchy of Lancaster
Authority:	The Merseyside Museums & Galleries Galleries Order 1986

Staff Numbers as at 1.4.87:		*Complement*	*In Post*
	Curatorial	43	41
	Warders	243	235
	Others	285	275
	TOTAL	571	551

			£
Grant-in-aid in 1988–89:	Running Costs		6,780,000
	Buildings		2,690,000
	Purchase Grant		750,000
	TOTAL		10,220,000

Attendance Figures (including branch museums) in 1987:	1,328,884

Main Buildings:	*Standard Admission Charge for Adults*
Liverpool Museum & Walker Art Gallery, William Brown Street, Liverpool	None
Maritime Museum, Pier Head, Liverpool	£1
Branch Museums:	
Lady Lever Art Gallery, Port Sunlight, Wirral	None
Museum of Labour History, William Brown Street, Liverpool	None
The Oratory	None
Sudley Art Gallery, Mossley Hill Road, Liverpool	None
Large Object Collection, Princes Dock, Liverpool	None

Appendix H **National Portrait Gallery**

The Gallery preserves and exhibits portraits of famous British men and women. It fulfils a triple function: as a series of public exhibition galleries, as a reference library of likenesses and as a research institute on British portraiture.

Date founded:	1856

Funding Department:	Office of Arts & Libraries

Governing Body:	Board of Trustees (16), appointed by the Prime Minister (14), ex officio (2)

Authority:	Treasury Minute 1856

Staff Numbers as at 1.4.87:		*Complement*	*In Post*
	Curatorial	25	25
	Warders	62	62
	Others	18	18
	TOTAL	105	105

		£
Grant-in-aid in 1988–89:	Running Costs	1,996,000
	Buildings	3,020,000
	Purchase Grant	310,000
	TOTAL	5,326,000

Attendance Figures (excluding branch museums) in 1987:	590,841

Main Building:	*Standard Admission Charge for Adults*
St Martins Place, London	None
Branch Museums:	
Beningbrough Hall, York	£1.90
Montacute House, Yeovil	£2.50
Bodelwyddan Castle, Clwyd (opening July 1988)	£2 (winter, £1.80)

Appendix I The Royal Air Force Museum

The collection focusses on the history of the Royal Air Force, presented in realistic reconstructions of historic settings. Forty aircraft are displayed, along with uniforms, paintings and navigation aids.

Date founded:	1963
Funding Department:	Ministry of Defence
Governing Body:	Board of Trustees (14), appointed by S of S for Defence
Authority:	Deed of Trust 1965

Staff Numbers as at 1.4.87:

	Complement	*In Post*
Curatorial	29	29
Warders	45	43
Others	40	31
TOTAL	114	103

Grant-in-aid in 1988–89:

	£
Running Costs	1,697,000
Buildings	—
Purchase Grant	59,000
TOTAL	1,756,000

Attendance Figures (including branch museum) in 1987: 317,000

Main Buildings: *Standard Admission Charge for Adults*

Hendon: Royal Air Force Museum
Hendon: Battle of Britain Museum   } £3
Hendon: Bomber Command Museum

Branch Museum:
Cosford Aerospace Museum, Wolverhampton   £2.25

Appendix J Royal Armouries

The Royal Armouries are the national collection of arms and armour.

Date founded:	*c.* 1680

Funding Department:	Department of the Environment

Governing Body:	Board of Trustees (6–11), appointed by the Sovereign (1), S of S for the Environment (remainder)

Authority:	National Heritage Act 1983

Staff Numbers as at 1.4.87:

	Complement	*In Post*
Curatorial	20	27
Warders	48	61
Others	13	21
TOTAL	81	109

Grant-in-aid in 1988–89:

	£
Running Costs	2,504,000
Buildings	501,000
Purchase Grant	295,000
TOTAL	3,300,000

Attendance Figures in 1987:	1,985,099 (87% of Tower of London attendance)

Main Building:	*Admission Charge*
Tower of London	(Admission is included in £3 admission charge to the Tower of London)

55

Appendix K **Science Museum**

The National Museum of Science & Industry holds the national collections on the history and contemporary practice of science, technology, industry, transport and medicine. There are three main outlets: the Science Museum, London; the National Railway Museum, York, and the National Museum of Photography, Film and Television, Bradford.

Date founded:	1857

Funding Department:	Office of Arts & Libraries

Governing Body:	Board of Trustees (12–20), appointed by the Prime Minister

Authority:	National Heritage Act 1983

Staff Numbers as at 1.4.87:		*Complement*	*In Post*
	Curatorial	182	168
	Warders	116	110
	Others	332	309
	TOTAL	630	587

Grant-in-aid in 1988–89:		£
	Running Costs	11,047,000
	Buildings	5,210,000
	Purchase Grant	375,000
	TOTAL	16,632,000

Attendance Figures (including branch museums) in 1987:	4,732,784

Main Building:	*Standard Admission Charge for Adults*
Science Museum, Exhibition Road, London	None

Branch Museums:

National Museum of Photography, Film & Television, Bradford	None
National Railway Museum, York	£1.50
Wroughton Airfield	£2 (average)
Concorde, Yeovilton	(Admission is included in £3 admission charge to the Fleet Air Arm Museum)

Appendix L Tate Gallery

The Tate Gallery comprises the national collection of British painting and 20th century painting and sculpture.

Date founded:	1897
Funding Department:	Office of Arts & Libraries
Governing Body:	Board of Trustees (11), appointed by the Prime Minister (10), National Gallery (1)
Authority:	Treasury letter of 24 March 1917 and the National Gallery and Tate Gallery Act 1954

Staff Numbers as at 1.4.87:		*Complement*	*In Post*
	Curatorial	85	73
	Warders	187	166
	Others	87	87
	TOTAL	359	326

Grant-in-aid in 1988–89:		£
	Running Costs	6,300,000
	Buildings	2,780,000
	Purchase Grant	1,815,000
	TOTAL	10,895,000

Attendance Figures (including branch museum) in 1987:	1,742,156

Main Building:
Millbank, London

Branch Museums:
Barbara Hepworth Museum, St Ives
Tate Gallery, Liverpool (opening May 1988)

Standard Admission Charge for Adults
None

50p
None

Appendix M Victoria & Albert Museum

The Museum holds and displays an international collection of the decorative arts, and is the National Museum of Art and Design.

Date founded:	1852

Funding Department:	Office of Arts & Libraries

Governing Body:	Board of Trustees (12–20), appointed by the Prime Minister

Authority:	National Heritage Act 1983

Staff Numbers as at 1.4.87:

		Complement	In Post
	Curatorial	158	152
	Warders	188	182
	Others	347	331
	TOTAL	693	665

		£
Grant-in-aid in 1988–89:	Running Costs	12,900,000
	Buildings	7,480,000
	Purchase Grant	1,145,000
	TOTAL	21,525,000

Attendance Figures (including branch museums) in 1987:	1,398,668

Main Building: *Standard Admission Charge for Adults*
Cromwell Road, London   (£2 suggested donation)

Branch Museums:

Apsley House (Wellington Museum), London	£2
Bethnal Green Museum of Childhood, London	None
Ham House, Richmond	£1.80
Osterley Park House, Middlesex	£1.80
Theatre Museum, London	£2.25

Appendix N Wallace Collection

The collection, bequeathed to the nation by Lady Wallace, comprises major paintings of the Italian, Dutch, Spanish, French and English schools, miniatures, sculpture, French 18th century furniture, goldsmiths' work, ceramics, glass, metalwork and European and oriental arms and armour. The terms of the bequest preclude acquisitions and loans.

Date founded:	1897

Funding Department:	Office of Arts & Libraries

Governing Body:	Board of Trustees (7), appointed by the Prime Minister

Authority:	Treasury Minute 1897

Staff Numbers as at 1.4.87:		*Complement*	*In Post*
	Curatorial	13	13
	Warders	56	56
	Others	7	7
	TOTAL	76	76

		£
Grant-in-aid in 1988–89:	Running Costs	1,149,000
	Buildings	449,000
	Purchase Grant	—
	TOTAL	1,598,000

Attendance Figures in 1987:	168,109

Main Building:	*Admission Charge*
Manchester Square, London	None

Appendix O National Galleries of Scotland

The National Galleries comprise the National Gallery of Scotland, the Scottish National Portrait Gallery and the Scottish National Gallery of Modern Art. They hold collections of national and international importance.

Date founded:	1850

Funding Department:	Scottish Education Department

Governing Body:	Board of Trustees (7–12), appointed by S of S for Scotland

Authority:	National Heritage (Scotland) Act 1985

Staff Numbers as at 1.4.87:		*Complement*	*In Post*
	Curatorial	24	23
	Warders	71	71
	Others	33	33
	TOTAL	128	127

Grant-in-aid in 1988–89:		£
	Running Costs	2,306,000
	Buildings	—
	Purchase Grant	1,578,000
	TOTAL	3,884,000

Attendance Figures (all buildings):	524,000

Main Buildings:	*Admission Charge*
National Gallery of Scotland, The Mound, Edinburgh	None
Scottish National Portrait Gallery, Queen Street, Edinburgh	None
Scottish National Gallery of Modern Art, Bedford Road, Edinburgh	None

Appendix P National Museums of Scotland

Comprehensive collections in two separate buildings: one embracing natural
history, oriental ceramics, Egyptian and primitive art, science and technology;
the other dedicated to the antiquities of Scotland, with Roman, Stuart and
Highland relics, costumes and textiles.

Date founded: 1780 (National Museum of Antiquities of
Scotland); 1854 (Royal Scottish Museum);
1985 (amalgamated as National Museums
of Scotland)

Funding Department: Scottish Education Department

Governing Body: Board of Trustees (9–15), appointed by
S of S for Scotland

Authority: National Heritage (Scotland) Act 1985

Staff Numbers as at 1.4.87:

	Complement	In Post
Curatorial	125	113
Warders	79	79
Others	55	55
TOTAL	259	247

Grant-in-aid in 1988–89:

	£
Running Costs	5,226,000
Buildings	—
Purchase Grant	642,000
TOTAL	5,868,000

Attendance Figures
(including branch museums) in 1987:   817,364

Main Buildings:

	Admission Charge
Chambers Street, Edinburgh	None
Queen Street, Edinburgh	None
Scottish United Services Museum, The Castle, Edinburgh	None

Branch Museums (closed during winter months):

Agricultural Museum, Ingliston	None
Biggar Gasworks Museum, Biggar	None
East Fortune Museum of Flight, North Berwick	None
Shambellie Museum of Costume, New Abbey	None

Appendix Q National Museum of Wales

With an emphasis on the history of Wales, the collections illustrate geology, botany, zoology and Welsh industry in addition to applied art and painting.

Date founded:	1907
Funding Department:	Welsh Office
Governing Body:	Court of Governors (188), appointed by S of S for Wales and others, and including various ex officio members
Authority:	Royal Charter 1911

Staff Numbers as at 1.4.87:

		Complement	*In Post*
Curatorial			109
Warders	(None fixed)		191
Others			116
TOTAL			416

Grant-in-aid in 1988–89:

	£
Running Costs	5,803,000
Buildings	3,997,000
Purchase Grant	1,199,000
TOTAL	10,999,000

Attendance Figures
(including branch museums) in 1987: 1,041,290

	Standard Admission Charge for Adults
Main Building:	
Cathays Park, Cardiff	None
Branch Museum:	
Welsh Folk Museum, St Fagan's	£2
Welsh Industrial and Maritime Museum, Cardiff	None
Museum of Welsh Woollen Industry, Drefach Felindre	None
Museum of North Wales, Llanberis	None
Roman Legionary Museum, Caerleon	75p
Segontium Roman Fort Museum, Caernarfon	None
Turner House, Penarth	None
Welsh Slate Museum, Llanberis	£1
Yr Hen Gapel	None

Appendix R Ulster Folk & Transport Museum

The collections illustrate the way of life and traditions of the people of Northern Ireland, with emphasis on transport by land, water and air.

Date founded:	1958
Funding Department:	Department of Education for Northern Ireland (DENI)
Governing Body:	Board of Trustees (15), appointed by Queen's University of Belfast (1), University of Ulster (1), Belfast City Council (2), District Councils (4), DENI (7)
Authority:	The Museums (Northern Ireland) Order 1981

Staff Numbers as at 1.4.87:

		Complement	*In Post*
Curatorial			19
Warders	(None fixed)		56
Others			73
TOTAL			148

Grant-in-aid in 1988–89:

		£
Running Costs		1,750,000
Buildings		102,000
Purchase Grant		87,000
TOTAL		1,939,000

Attendance Figures
(including branch museum) in 1987:   193,653

Main Building:	*Standard Admission Charge for Adults*
Cultra Manor, Holywood, Co Down	£1
Branch Museum:	
Witham Street, Belfast	30p

Appendix S **Ulster Museum**

The collections are divided into five departments: Antiquities, Art, Botany and Zoology, Geology and Local History (including Industrial Archaeology). There are also Departments of Conservation, of Design and Exhibition Services and of Museums Services.

Date founded:	1831 (as national museum, 1961)
Funding Department:	Department of Eduction for Northern Ireland (DENI)
Governing Body:	Board of Trustees (15), appointed by Queen's University of Belfast (1), University of Ulster (1), Belfast City Council (3), District Councils (3), DENI (7)
Authority:	The Museums (Northern Ireland) Order 1981

Staff Numbers as at 1.4.87:

		Complement	*In Post*
	Curatorial	43	41
	Warders	69	66
	Others	57	50
	TOTAL	169	157

Grant-in-aid in 1988–89:

		£
	Running Costs	2,291,000
	Buildings	182,000
	Purchase Grant	167,000
	TOTAL	2,640,000

Attendance Figures (including branch museum) in 1987:	276,865

Main Building:	*Admission Charge*
Botanic Gardens, Belfast	None
Branch Museum:	
Armagh County Museum	None

Printed in the United Kingdom for Her Majesty's Stationery Office
Dd 240061   4/88   C15   443/5   59471